WORLD SOCCER CLUBS

MANCHESTER UNITED

by David J. Clarke

Copyright © 2025 by Press Room Editions. All rights reserved. No part of this book may be used or reproduced in any manner whatsoever, including internet usage, without written permission from the copyright owner, except in the case of brief quotations embodied in critical articles and reviews.

Book design by Kate Liestman
Cover design by Kate Liestman

Photographs ©: Andrew Mordzynski/Icon Sportswire/AP Images, cover; Alex Pantling/Getty Images Sport/Getty Images, 5; Alex Livesey/Danehouse/Getty Images Sport/Getty Images, 7; Mike Hewitt/Getty Images Sport/Getty Images, 9; Wirestock Creators/Shutterstock, 11; Matthews/Daily Express/Hulton Archive/Getty Images, 13; EMPPL PA Wire/AP Images, 15; Fox Photos/Hulton Archive/Getty Images, 17; Evening Standard/Hulton Archive/Getty Images, 19; Calvert/AP Images, 21; Gary M. Prior/Allsport/Getty Images Sport/Getty Images, 23; Ben Radford/Allsport/Hulton Archive/Getty Images, 25; Ross Kinnaird/Getty Images Sport/Getty Images, 27; Clive Brunskill/Getty Images Sport/Getty Images, 29

Press Box Books, an imprint of Press Room Editions.

ISBN
978-1-63494-961-3 (library bound)
978-1-63494-975-0 (paperback)
979-8-89469-006-3 (epub)
978-1-63494-989-7 (hosted ebook)

Library of Congress Control Number: 2024940901

Distributed by North Star Editions, Inc.
2297 Waters Drive
Mendota Heights, MN 55120
www.northstareditions.com

Printed in the United States of America
012025

ABOUT THE AUTHOR

David J. Clarke is a freelance sportswriter. Originally from Helena, Montana, he now lives in Savannah, Georgia.

TABLE OF CONTENTS

CHAPTER 1
TALENTED TEENS 4

CHAPTER 2
THE BUSBY BABES 10

CHAPTER 3
REBUILDING A CHAMPION 16

CHAPTER 4
A PREMIER TEAM 22

SUPERSTAR PROFILE
WAYNE ROONEY 28

QUICK STATS 30
GLOSSARY 31
TO LEARN MORE . . . 32
INDEX 32

CHAPTER 1

TALENTED TEENS

Manchester United midfielder Kobbie Mainoo drifted into the penalty area. On the right wing, Alejandro Garnacho looked to make a pass. Both players were just 19 years old. Garnacho passed the ball to United captain Bruno Fernandes. The midfielder had a chance to shoot. Instead, he slid a pass to Mainoo.

Alejandro Garnacho recorded 10 goals and five assists for Manchester United during the 2023–24 season.

The teenager tapped it in. Suddenly, Manchester United led rival Manchester City 2–0 in the 2024 FA Cup final.

The two teams had been playing each other since 1881. Manchester United had dominated much of that history. In the 1990s and 2000s, no team in England could match United. Manchester City struggled to keep up with the success of its local rival.

However, that started to change in the 2010s. Entering the 2023–24 season, United had won the FA Cup only once in 19 years. Meanwhile, City had become one of the world's best teams. Just one year earlier, City had won the English Premier League and the European

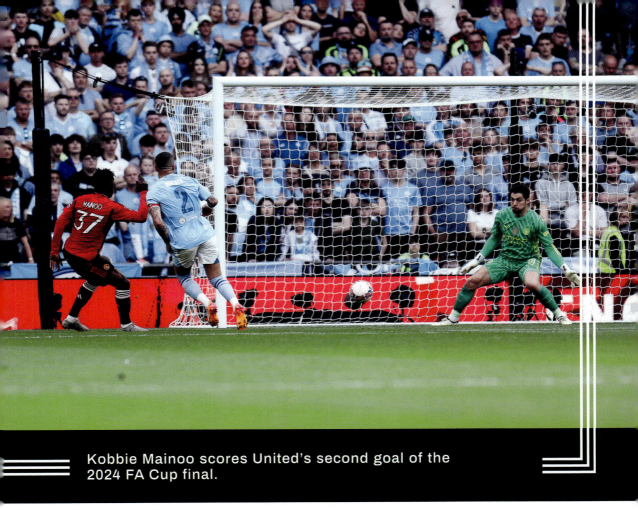

Kobbie Mainoo scores United's second goal of the 2024 FA Cup final.

Champions League. City had also beaten United in the 2023 FA Cup final.

United entered the 2024 final as an underdog. But the Red Devils stunned City in the first half. Garnacho pounced on a sloppy City pass in the 30th minute.

He then scored on an open net. Mainoo added his goal nine minutes later. It was the first time two teenagers had scored in the FA Cup final. The goals gave United fans hope that their team could win.

It still wasn't easy. Manchester City's attack stepped it up in the second half. One shot hit the crossbar. United goalkeeper André Onana made a diving save on another. Manchester City scored

YOUTH MOVEMENT

Kobbie Mainoo and Alejandro Garnacho joined superstar company in the 2024 FA Cup final. The last teenager to score in an FA Cup final had been Cristiano Ronaldo. The forward had tallied a goal for Manchester United in the 2004 final. His goal helped United win 3–0.

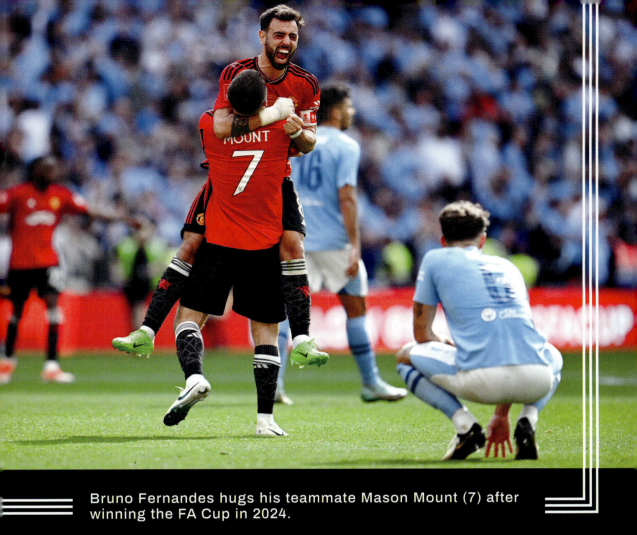

Bruno Fernandes hugs his teammate Mason Mount (7) after winning the FA Cup in 2024.

a late goal. But United held on for a 2–1 win. The upset victory thrilled Manchester United fans. Young stars such as Mainoo and Garnacho were leading the club back to glory.

CHAPTER 2

THE BUSBY BABES

In 1878, employees of the Lancashire and Yorkshire Railway (LYR) formed a new soccer club. They called it Newton Heath LYR Football Club. It would go on to become England's most successful team.

However, the club's early years were rough. By 1902, the team had run out of money. A group of local

Manchester United's stadium, Old Trafford, is located just outside of Manchester.

businesspeople stepped in to save the club. They bought the team. Then they renamed it Manchester United.

By 1911, the team had won two English league titles. But after that, the club went decades without a championship. In 1945, the club hired Matt Busby as its new manager. Busby decided he would try to recruit young stars.

The strategy began to pay off by the early 1950s. United entered the final day of the 1951–52 season three points ahead of Arsenal. The teams faced off for the championship. United striker Jack Rowley scored a hat trick. Manchester United won 6–1. That gave United its first championship in 41 years.

Matt Busby managed Manchester United for 25 seasons.

By the end of the 1956–57 season, the club had added two league titles. Busby's young players were called the "Busby Babes." In 1956–57, the club became the first English team to play in the European Cup. That competition featured the best

13

teams in Europe. Today it's known as the Champions League.

Manchester United played in the tournament again the following season. The team was traveling home from Munich, Germany, in February 1958. United's plane crashed while taking off. Of the 44 people on board, 23 died. Eight were players. Two other players suffered

OLD TRAFFORD

Old Trafford opened in 1910. Manchester United has played home games there ever since. The stadium originally held 80,000 fans. It can now hold 74,310. Old Trafford is the largest club stadium in England. In the 1960s, United midfielder Bobby Charlton nicknamed it the "Theater of Dreams."

Goalkeeper Harry Gregg was one of the survivors of the plane crash in Munich. He played in 231 matches for Manchester United.

career-ending injuries. The crash had destroyed England's best team. Busby survived after spending nine weeks in the hospital. He then returned to Manchester United. But he had to rebuild his shattered team.

CHAPTER 3

REBUILDING A CHAMPION

Bobby Charlton survived the plane crash in Munich. The midfielder was 20 years old in 1958. Once Charlton could play again, Matt Busby had a new young star to build around. Charlton blasted hard shots and could score from all over the field. He soon became the best player in England.

Bobby Charlton scored 249 goals for Manchester United.

Charlton couldn't get Manchester United back on top by himself, though. In 1962, Busby signed forward Denis Law. The duo of Charlton and Law helped United win the FA Cup in 1963. Then striker George Best joined the senior team from United's youth academy. Best, Charlton, and Law were dubbed the "Holy Trinity." The legendary trio led United to the league title during the 1964–65 season.

THE RED DEVILS

In the 1960s, Matt Busby wanted a tougher nickname for his team than the "Busby Babes." A local rugby team called itself the Red Devils. Busby borrowed the name. Manchester United still goes by that name today. The team's uniform even features a devil patch.

Denis Law scored 28 league goals for Manchester United during the 1964–65 season.

The Red Devils won the English league again in 1966–67. The victory qualified them for the European Cup. No English team had ever won that tournament. In the semifinals, Manchester United defeated Spanish powerhouse Real Madrid. The

Red Devils then played Portuguese champions Benfica in the final.

   The game was tied 1–1 heading into extra time. Just three minutes into extra time, Best raced after a loose ball. A Benfica defender sprinted for it. Best got there first. He flipped the ball toward the goal. The Benfica goalkeeper came charging out. Best reached the ball first. He then chopped it back the other direction. Best tapped the ball into the open net. After that, United scored two more goals. The 4–1 win gave the club its first European trophy. Busby's rebuild was complete. Ten years earlier, Manchester United had suffered tragedy. Now, the club was the best in Europe.

George Best scores on an open net during the 1968 European Cup final.

Busby retired in 1971. After he stopped coaching the team, Manchester United started to fade. The team even got relegated after the 1973–74 season. For the next decade, United fought to get back to its winning ways. It would take another amazing manager to turn things around.

CHAPTER 4

A PREMIER TEAM

In the summer of 1986, Manchester United hired Alex Ferguson as manager. His first few seasons didn't go well. By 1990, many United fans wanted him fired. Ferguson's teams started winning just in time. In 1992, the top English teams formed the Premier League. The new league

David Beckham scored 27 goals from free kicks while he played for Manchester United.

had a lot of money. Winning the title could make a team rich.

United won the Premier League four times in the competition's first five years. The team featured stars such as midfielders David Beckham and Ryan Giggs. In 1998–99, United won the Premier League again. The club also won the FA Cup. Then United took on Bayern Munich in the Champions League final.

No English team had ever won three major competitions in one season before. It didn't look like United would, either. The Red Devils trailed 1–0 in stoppage time. Then forward Teddy Sheringham scored following a corner kick. Moments later, United earned another corner. Sheringham

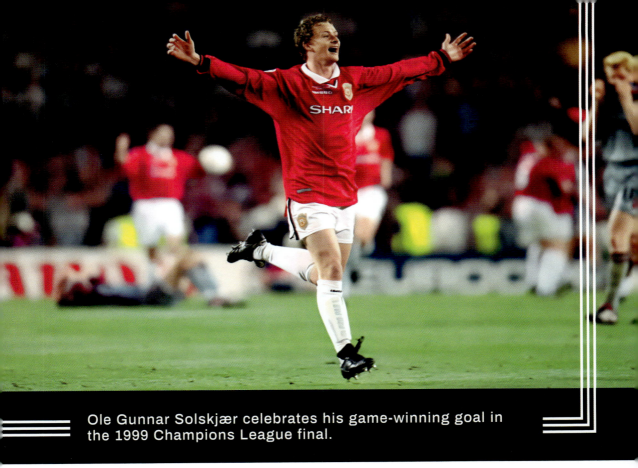

Ole Gunnar Solskjær celebrates his game-winning goal in the 1999 Champions League final.

flicked the ball to the back post. Substitute Ole Gunnar Solskjær stuck his leg out and poked the ball in. The traveling United fans erupted. Their team had pulled off a miracle to make history.

Ferguson soon signed new stars. By the mid-2000s, Wayne Rooney and Cristiano

Ronaldo were United's key attackers. They led the club to the Champions League final again in 2008. The Red Devils beat English rival Chelsea in a shootout.

Ferguson retired after winning his 13th Premier League title in 2012–13. He had been with the team for 27 years. Manchester United struggled to replace

THE CLASS OF '92

In 1992, six players graduated to the senior team from Manchester United's academy. David Beckham became a global superstar. Ryan Giggs eventually appeared in more Manchester United games than any other player. Midfielders Paul Scholes and Nicky Butt became club legends. So did defenders Gary and Phil Neville. These players are known as the "Class of '92."

Many soccer fans consider Cristiano Ronaldo (right) to be one of the greatest players of all time.

him. Over the next decade, the team went through several managers. Through the early 2020s, none were able to win the Premier League. However, winning the FA Cup in 2024 gave fans hope that United could return to glory.

SUPERSTAR PROFILE

WAYNE ROONEY

Wayne Rooney joined Manchester United in 2004. At the time, he was just 18 years old. The teenager had already played in the Premier League with Everton. In fact, he was the youngest goal scorer in league history.

Rooney kept scoring after he joined United. He recorded a hat trick in his first appearance for the club. Rooney stayed with Manchester United until 2017. By that point, he had scored 183 Premier League goals for the club. At the time, no player had scored more Premier League goals for one team.

Rooney had quickness and strength. He could unleash hard and accurate shots. But his work ethic set him apart. It helped him stay at the top of his game when he got older.

Rooney's 253 total goals are the most in Manchester United history. He also helped the team win. Rooney's teams won the Premier League five times. He also won a Champions League title and an FA Cup.

Wayne Rooney recorded 139 assists during his career with Manchester United.

QUICK STATS

MANCHESTER UNITED

Founded: 1878

Home stadium: Old Trafford

English league titles: 20

European Cup/Champions League titles: 3

FA Cup titles: 13

Key managers:

- Ernest Mangnall (1903–12): 2 English league titles, 1 FA Cup title

- Matt Busby (1945–69, 1970–71): 5 English league titles, 2 FA Cup titles, 1 European Cup title

- Alex Ferguson (1986–2013): 13 Premier League titles, 5 FA Cup titles, 2 Champions League titles

Most career appearances: Ryan Giggs (961)

Most career goals: Wayne Rooney (253)

Stats are accurate through the 2023–24 season.

GLOSSARY

academy
A program set up by a professional soccer club to develop young players.

extra time
Two 15-minute halves that take place if a knockout game is tied after 90 minutes of play.

hat trick
When a player scores three or more goals in a game.

penalty area
The 18-yard box in front of the goal where a player is granted a penalty kick if he or she is fouled.

relegated
Sent down to a lower league because of a bad record.

rival
An opposing player or team that brings out the greatest emotion from fans and players.

shootout
A way of deciding a tie game. Players from each team take a series of penalty kicks.

stoppage time
Time added to the end of a soccer match to account for stoppages in play.

underdog
A player or team that is not expected to win.

TO LEARN MORE

Bischer, Karen. *Cristiano Ronaldo vs. Lionel Messi: Soccer Legends Face Off*. North Mankato, MN: Capstone Press, 2025.

Donnelly, Patrick. *The Best Managers of World Soccer*. Minneapolis: Abdo Publishing, 2024.

Hewson, Anthony K. *GOATs of Soccer*. North Mankato, MN: Abdo Publishing, 2022.

MORE INFORMATION

To learn more about Manchester United, go to **pressboxbooks.com/AllAccess**. These links are routinely monitored and updated to provide the most current information available.

INDEX

Beckham, David, 24, 26
Best, George, 18, 20
Busby, Matt, 12–13, 15, 16, 18, 20–21
Butt, Nicky, 26

Charlton, Bobby, 14, 16, 18

Ferguson, Alex, 22, 25–26
Fernandes, Bruno, 4

Garnacho, Alejandro, 4, 7–9
Giggs, Ryan, 24, 26

Law, Denis, 18

Mainoo, Kobbie, 4, 6, 8–9

Neville, Gary, 26
Neville, Phil, 26

Onana, André, 8

Ronaldo, Cristiano, 8, 25–26
Rooney, Wayne, 25–26, 28
Rowley, Jack, 12

Scholes, Paul, 26
Sheringham, Teddy, 24
Solskjær, Ole Gunnar, 25